QUOTES

OF

BEYONCE

Inspirational and motivational quotations of Beyonce Knowles

Terms Of Use Agreement

Every effort had been made to fulfill requirements with regard to reproducing copyrighted material. The author and the publisher will be glad to certify any omissions at the earliest opportunity.

Disclaimer

The author and the publisher have used their best efforts in preparing this book. The author and the publisher make no representation or warranties with respect to the accuracy, fitness, applicability, or completeness of the contents of this work and specifically disclaim all warranties, including without limitation warranties of fitness for a particular purpose. This work is sold with the understanding that author and the publisher is not engaged in rendering legal, or any other professional services.

The information contained in this book is strictly for educational purposes. Therefore, if you wish to apply ideas contained within this book, you are taking full responsibility for your actions. The author and the publisher disclaim any warranties (express or implied), merchantability, or fitness for any particular purpose.

Beyonce Knowles Quotes

If everything was perfect, you would never learn and you would never grow.
— Beyonce Knowles

When you love and accept yourself, when you know who really cares about you, and when you learn from your mistakes, then you stop caring about what people who don't know you think.
— Beyonce Knowles

I think it's healthy for a person to be nervous. It means you care - that you work hard and want to give a great performance. You just have to channel that nervous energy into the show.
— Beyonce Knowles

The great thing about McDonald's is that they have a lot of different things on the menu. I love their salads.
— Beyonce Knowles

I think music is something that can, and should, be used to get you into different things because eventually

what goes up must come down - we're not going to be the number one group in the world forever - so you have to have something else to fall back on.
— Beyonce Knowles

Who I am on stage is very, very different to who I am in real life.
— Beyonce Knowles

I always treat myself to one meal on Sundays when I can have whatever I want. Usually it's pizza, which is my favorite indulgence.
— Beyonce Knowles

I love a pair of sexy heels with jeans, a nice jacket, or a little dress.
— Beyonce Knowles

For me, it's about the way I carry myself and the way I treat other people. My relationship and how I feel about God and what He does for me, is something deeply personal. It's where I came from, my family, I was brought up in a religious household and that's very important to me.

— Beyonce Knowles

I can never be safe; I always try and go against the grain. As soon as I accomplish one thing, I just set a higher goal. That's how I've gotten to where I am.

— Beyonce Knowles

I hold a lot of things in. I'm always making sure everybody is okay. I usually don't rage; I usually don't curse. So for me, it's a great thing to be able to scream and say whatever I want.

— Beyonce Knowles

We all have special numbers in our lives, and 4 is that for me. It's the day I was born. My mother's birthday, and a lot of my friends' birthdays, are on the fourth; April 4 is my wedding date.

— Beyonce Knowles

I feel like you get more bees with honey. But that doesn't mean I don't get frustrated in my life. My way

of dealing with frustration is to shut down and to think and speak logically.
— Beyonce Knowles

Tina Turner is someone that I admire, because she made her strength feminine and sexy. Marilyn Monroe, because she was a curvy woman. I'm drawn to things that have the same kind of silhouettes as what she wore because our bodies are similar.
— Beyonce Knowles

I don't really like to call myself a brand, and I don't like to think of myself as a brand. I'm a singer, a songwriter, a musician and a performer. And an actress, and all the other things that I do. When you add it all together, some might call it a brand, but that's not my focus.
— Beyonce Knowles

I discovered after going to music festivals that I am a rock fan. I love the guitars, the phrasing, and the abandon of rock fans.
— Beyonce Knowles

I get nervous when I don't get nervous. If I'm nervous I know I'm going to have a good show.
— Beyonce Knowles

My fans kept asking where they could get clothes like 'Destiny's Child's', so it was only natural for us to do a clothing line. I was adamant about not putting my name on something that I didn't love.
— Beyonce Knowles

My focus is my art, and that's what I love to do. I have to be really passionate in order to do something. I've turned down many things that I just didn't believe in.
— Beyonce Knowles

My fans kept asking where they could get clothes like Destiny's Child's, so it was only natural for us to do a clothing line.
— Beyonce Knowles

Power means happiness; power means hard work and sacrifice.
— Beyonce Knowles

We all have our imperfections. But I'm human, and you know, it's important to concentrate on other qualities besides outer beauty.
— Beyonce Knowles

I wanted to sell a million records, and I sold a million records. I wanted to go platinum; I went platinum. I've been working nonstop since I was 15. I don't even know how to chill out.
— Beyonce Knowles

Whenever I'm confused about something, I ask God to reveal the answers to my questions, and he does.
— Beyonce Knowles

When you really don't like a guy, they're all over you, and as soon as you act like you like them, they're no longer interested.
— Beyonce Knowles

I truly believe that women should be financially independent from their men. And let's face it, money gives men the power to run the show. It gives men the

power to define value. They define what's sexy. And men define what's feminine. It's ridiculous.
— Beyonce Knowles

I remember being in Japan when Destiny's Child put out 'Independent Women,' and women there were saying how proud they were to have their own jobs, their own independent thinking, their own goals. It made me feel so good, and I realized that one of my responsibilities was to inspire women in a deeper way.
— Beyonce Knowles

I'm a human being and I fall in love and sometimes I don't have control of every situation.
— Beyonce Knowles

If I weren't performing, I'd be a beauty editor or a therapist. I love creativity, but I also love to help others. My mother was a hairstylist, and they listen to everyone's problems - like a beauty therapist!
— Beyonce Knowles

I'm over being a pop star. I don't wanna be a hot girl. I wanna be iconic. And I feel like I've accomplished a lot.

I feel like I'm highly respected, which is more important than any award or any amount of records. And I feel like there comes a point when being a pop star is not enough.
— Beyonce Knowles

I always have breakfast, say, scrambled egg whites, a vegetable smoothie, or whole-grain cereal with low-fat milk. For lunch and dinner, I eat a lot of fish and vegetables. And throughout the day, I try to stay hydrated.
— Beyonce Knowles

I've worn dresses from all different price ranges, and the thing that couture dresses have in common is that the fit is amazing.
— Beyonce Knowles

I like to walk around with bare feet and I don't like to comb my hair.
— Beyonce Knowles

The more successful I become, the more I need a man.
— Beyonce Knowles

I mean, I feel like you get more bees with honey. But that doesn't mean I don't get frustrated in my life.
— Beyonce Knowles

When I was writing the Destiny's Child songs, it was a big thing to be that young and taking control. And the label at the time didn't know that we were going to be that successful, so they gave us all control. And I got used to it.
— Beyonce Knowles

I'm a people pleaser. I hold a lot of things in. I'm always making sure everybody is okay. I usually don't rage; I usually don't curse.
— Beyonce Knowles

Y'all are so cute and y'all talk so proper over here. I love England.
— Beyonce Knowles

In my videos, I always want to be a powerful woman. That's my mission.
— Beyonce Knowles

There's my personal life, my sensitive side, and then
me as a performer, sexy and energised and fun.
— Beyonce Knowles

I know I'm stronger in the songs than I really am.
Sometimes I need to hear it myself. We all need to hear
those empowering songs to remind us.
— Beyonce Knowles

I grew up upper-class. Private school. My dad had a
Jaguar. We're African-American, and we work together
as a family, so people assume we're like the Jacksons.
But I didn't have parents using me to get out of a bad
situation.
— Beyonce Knowles

My style offstage is so different from onstage. I love a
pair of sexy heels with jeans, a nice jacket, or a little
dress.
— Beyonce Knowles

If he invited you out, he's got to pay.
— Beyonce Knowles

Diana Ross is a big inspiration to all of us. We all grew up watching everything about her - her mike placement, her grace, her style and her class.
— Beyonce Knowles

You know what, I'm very attracted to someone who makes me laugh and is that charming. Really, I could be charmed by anyone. I'm just a sucker for somebody that is charming.
— Beyonce Knowles

I always try to be myself. Ever since I was an introverted kid, I'd get on stage and be able to break out of my shell.
— Beyonce Knowles

I grew up in a very nice house in Houston, went to private school all my life and I've never even been to the 'hood. Not that there's anything wrong with the 'hood.
— Beyonce Knowles

I just hope people don't get sick of us. I'm sick of us
and I'm in Destiny's Child.
— Beyonce Knowles

One of the reasons I connect to the Super Bowl is that I
approach my shows like an athlete.
— Beyonce Knowles

To be able to travel the world, especially to places I
never thought I'd be... it's really, you know, still
fascinating for me.
— Beyonce Knowles

I just try to write songs that people are going to have a
dialogue about.
— Beyonce Knowles

I love my job, but it's more than that: I need it.
— Beyonce Knowles

Any other woman who has to go to work and pick up
the kids and make dinner - that's way harder than what
I have to do.
— Beyonce Knowles

I am really proud that I am one of the artists that has the opportunity to be on magazine covers and to be in the movies.
— Beyonce Knowles

I wanted to be famous for my music and my talent, and I always wished I could cut it out when I left the stage.
— Beyonce Knowles

Tina Turner is someone that I admire, because she made her strength feminine and sexy.
— Beyonce Knowles

We're African-American and we work together as a family, so people assume we're like the Jacksons. But I didn't have parents using me to get out of a bad situation.
— Beyonce Knowles

When you're a pop star, it's a little conservative; you always have to stay in a box. You have fans that are

five and fans that are 65; there are so many people wanting so many things.
— Beyonce Knowles

Playing Etta James in the movie 'Cadillac Records' really changed me. It was a darker character, and I realized that if anything is too comfortable, I want to run from it. It's no fun being safe.
— Beyonce Knowles

There are a lot of things I never did, because I believe in watching those true Hollywood stories and I see how easy it is to lose track of your life.
— Beyonce Knowles

Your self-worth is determined by you. You don't have to depend on someone telling you who you are.
— Beyonce Knowles

Lady Gaga might be the sweetest, sweetest angel ever.
— Beyonce Knowles

The more successful I become, the more I need a man.
— Beyonce Knowles

I put my heart in that album (Dangerously In Love). After playing the songs for my record label, they told me I didn't have one hit on my album. Dangerously In Love, Naughty Girl, Me Myself & I, Baby Boy and my favorite; Crazy In Love. But they told me I didn't have one hit on my album. I guess they were kind of right. I had five!
— Beyonce Knowles

I don't like to gamble, but if there's one thing I'm willing to bet on, it's myself.
— Beyonce Knowles

I only allow myself one day to feel sorry for myself. People who complain really get on my nerves. When I'm not feeling my best I ask myself, 'What are you gonna do about it?' I use the negativity to fuel the transformation into a better me.
— Beyonce Knowles

Take all the rules away. How can we live if we don't change?
— Beyonce Knowles

When I think of the time that I almost loved you, you showed your ass, and I saw the real you.
— Beyonce Knowles

There's ups and downs in this love. Got a lot to learn in this love. Through the good and the bad, still got love.
— Beyonce Knowles

When I leave this world, I'll leave no regrets. Leave something to remember, so they won't forget I was here.
— Beyonce Knowles

I'm over being a pop-star. I don't want to be a hot girl. I want to be iconic.
— Beyonce Knowles

If you are with the right person, it brings out the best version of you.
— Beyonce Knowles

I'm a human being and I fall in love and sometimes I don't have control of every situation.
— Beyonce Knowles

When you really don't like a guy, they're all over you, and as soon as you act like you like them, they're no longer interested.
— Beyonce Knowles

You're the only one I wish I could forget, the only one I love to not forgive.
— Beyonce Knowles

You're everything I thought you never were and nothing like I thought you could've been.
— Beyonce Knowles

There are times that I hate you 'cause I can't erase the times that you hurt me and put tears on my face.
— Beyonce Knowles

With a lot of success comes a lot of negativity.
— Beyonce Knowles

Boy, you my temporary high.
— Beyonce Knowles

You can be a sweet dream or a beautiful nightmare. Either way, I don't want to wake up from you.
— Beyonce Knowles

Still all up on each other, ain't a damn thing changed. My girls can't tell me nothin', I'm gone in the brain.
— Beyonce Knowles

Don't be mad when she finally lets go and ends up with someone who actually gives a damn about her.
— Beyonce Knowles

In the quest for love, we are all trying to find that perfect someone. Someone who cherishes you, someone who loves you for you, and loves you as much as you love them.
— Beyonce Knowles

I'm a workaholic and I don't believe in 'No'. If I'm not sleeping, nobody's sleeping.
— Beyonce Knowles

If you wanna keep me all you have to do is hold me, squeeze me, tease me, please me, dress me, undress me, and baby, I'll be there!
— Beyonce Knowles

Trust is like a mirror; you can't fix it when it's broken.
— Beyonce Knowles

When I'm not feeling my best I ask myself, 'What are you gonna do about it?' I use the negativity to fuel the transformation into a better me.
— Beyonce Knowles Knowles

"Your self-worth is determined by you. You don't have to depend on someone telling you who you are."
— Beyonce Knowles

"I'm over being a pop star. I don't wanna be a hot girl. I wanna be iconic."
— Beyonce Knowles

"The most alluring thing a woman can have is confidence."
— Beyonce Knowles

"I felt like it was time to set up my future, so I set a goal. My goal was independence."
— Beyonce Knowles

"My message behind this album was finding the beauty in imperfection."
— Beyonce Knowles

"We need to reshape our own perception of how we view ourselves. We have to step up as women and take the lead."
— Beyonce Knowles

"I am a woman and when I think, I must speak."
— Beyonce Knowles

"Power's not given to you. You have to take it."
— Beyonce Knowles

"Take all the rules away. How can we live if we don't change?"
— Beyonce Knowles

"Perfection is a disease of a nation."
— Beyonce Knowles

"I guess I am a modern-day feminist. I do believe in equality. Why do you have to choose what type of woman you are? Why do you have to label yourself anything?"
— Beyonce Knowles

"When I'm not feeling my best I ask myself, 'What are you gonna do about it?' I use the negativity to fuel the transformation into a better me."
— Beyonce Knowles

"I'm a workaholic and I don't believe in 'no.' If I'm not sleeping, nobody's sleeping."
— Beyonce Knowles

"He will change diapers, of course he will. He is going to be a very hands-on father."
— Beyonce Knowles

"The reality is: sometimes you lose. And you're never too good to lose. You're never too big to lose. You're never too smart to lose. It happens."
— Beyonce Knowles

"Your self-worth is determined by you. You don't have to depend on someone telling you who you are."
— Beyonce Knowles

"When I'm not feeling my best I ask myself, 'What are you gonna do about it?' I use the negativity to fuel the transformation into a better me."
— Beyonce Knowles

"Take all the rules away. How can we live if we don't change?"
— Beyonce Knowles

"I'm a workaholic and I don't believe in 'No'. If I'm not sleeping, nobody's sleeping."
— Beyonce Knowles

"Do what you were born to do. You just have to trust yourself."
— Beyonce Knowles

"I felt like it was time to set up my future, so I set a goal. My goal was independence."
— Beyonce Knowles

"Why do you have to choose what type of woman you are? Why do you have to label yourself anything?"
— Beyonce Knowles

"The reality is: sometimes you lose. And you're never too good to lose. You're never too big to lose. You're never too smart to lose. It happens."
— Beyonce Knowles

"I don't have to prove anything to anyone, I only have to follow my heart and concentrate on what I want to say to the world. I run my world."
— Beyonce Knowles

"It is so liberating to really know what I want, what truly makes me happy, what I will not tolerate. I have

learned that it is no one else's job to take care of me
but me."
— Beyonce Knowles

"[A true diva is] graceful, and talented, and strong, and
fearless and brave and someone with humility."
— Beyonce Knowles

"My biggest thing is to teach not to focus on the
aesthetic. It's really about who you are, and the human
being, that makes you beautiful."
— Beyonce Knowles

"We all have our imperfections. But I'm human and you
know, it's important to concentrate on other qualities
besides outer beauty."
— Beyonce Knowles

"The more you mature, you realize that this
imperfections make your more beautiful."
— Beyonce Knowles

"I don't like to gamble, but if there's one thing I'm willing to bet on, it's myself."
— Beyonce Knowles

"I don't feel like I have to please anyone. I feel free. I feel like I'm an adult. I'm grown. I can do what I want. I can say what I want. I can retire if I want. That's why I've worked hard."
— Beyonce Knowles

"If you've been doing all you can and it's not happening for you, go out and have you a good old time. Put on your sexy dress and move on."
— Beyonce Knowles

"Do what you were born to do. You just have to trust yourself."
— Beyonce Knowles

"If everything was perfect, you would never learn and you would never grow."
— Beyonce Knowles

"I'm a workaholic and I don't believe in 'no.' If I'm not sleeping, nobody's sleeping."
— Beyonce Knowles

"[A true diva is] graceful, and talented, and strong, and fearless and brave and someone with humility."
— Beyonce Knowles

"We all have our imperfections. But I'm human and you know, it's important to concentrate on other qualities besides outer beauty."
— Beyonce Knowles

"I am a woman and when I think, I must speak.
— Beyonce Knowles"

"I truly believe that women should be financially independent from their men. And let's face it, money gives men the power to run the show. It gives men the power to define value. They define what's sexy. And men define what's feminine. It's ridiculous."
— Beyonce Knowles

"When I'm not feeling my best I ask myself, 'What are you gonna do about it?' I use the negativity to fuel the transformation into a better me."
— Beyonce Knowles

"The reality is: sometimes you lose. And you're never too good to lose. You're never too big to lose. You're never too smart to lose. It happens."
— Beyonce Knowles

"I don't have to prove anything to anyone, I only have to follow my heart and concentrate on what I want to say to the world. I run my world."
— Beyonce Knowles

"I guess I am a modern-day feminist. I do believe in equality. Why do you have to choose what type of woman you are? Why do you have to label yourself anything?"
— Beyonce Knowles

CPSIA information can be obtained
at www.ICGtesting.com
Printed in the USA
LVOW13s2132120417
530639LV00011B/611/P